MINOR RAIl

A complete list of all
Standard Gauge, Narrow Gauge, Miniature,
Cliff Railways & Tramways in the British Isles

36th EDITION – 2024

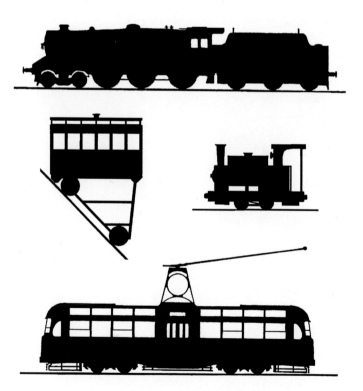

PETER SCOTT

Minor Railways Web Site

Visit the **Minor Railways** web site.
Supplement: Continuously updated supplement.
News: All the news about new lines, extensions & closures.
Publications: A list of books from the publisher of **MINOR RAILWAYS**.
Research: Appeals for information and a database resource facility.
Links: Links to other Societies and to all known Minor Railway web sites.
Track Plans: Downloadable track plans of Minor Railways. *
Histories: Illustrated articles on Minor Railway history.

* Under development

www.minorrailways.co.uk

MINOR RAILWAYS
A complete list of all Standard Gauge, Narrow Gauge, Miniature, Cliff Railways & Tramways in the British Isles

36th EDITION - 2024

ISBN 978 1 902368 55 9

Published by **Peter Scott**
93 Josephine Court, Southcote Road, Reading, RG30 2DQ
E-Mail: scott.pe@btinternet.com. Web Site: www.minorrailways.co.uk

MINOR RAILWAYS is compiled and published by Peter Scott at the address shown above. It is supplied free to members of the *Branch Line Society*, details of which are shown on page 35. Corrections and updates to *MINOR RAILWAYS*, and any comments about the contents, should be sent to the Compiler.

INTRODUCTION

MINOR RAILWAYS lists all known Standard Gauge, Narrow Gauge, Miniature, Cliff Railways and Tramways, offering rides to the general public, that are operated mainly for leisure purposes (as opposed to commercial transport operations). Lines that are out of use, under construction or proposed are not included. Each line has a separate entry to show: name, location, gauge, layout, length, OS grid reference and telephone number. The list is divided into four sections as shown in the list of Contents below.

Please note the information contained in this book is provided in good faith and whilst every effort has been made to make the contents as accurate as possible, no liability can be accepted for any errors or omissions.

CONTENTS

Each main section has its own introductory page

SUPPLEMENTS

To enable the list to keep up with the ever changing world of minor railways, it is intended to produce three supplements to appear in late May, early August and at the end of October. Branch Line Society members will be supplied these via *Branch Line News*. Any non-members wishing to obtain supplements should e-mail or write to the Compiler. Supplements can also be downloaded as pdf files from the **Minor Railways** web site or obtained by e-mail request from the Compiler. Alternatively, view the Online Supplement, which is updated continuously - go to: www.minorrailways.co.uk/supplement.php.

OPERATING DATES & TIMES

For the majority of railways, telephone numbers are shown to enable readers to find the operating dates and times of the railway(s) they wish to visit. Note that some of these are for evening use only - please be sensible and do not ring these numbers late in the evening. Telephone numbers are only given here where they have been previously publicly advertised elsewhere. Where no telephone number is available, brief operating details are given. For those who have Internet access, the **Minor Railways** web site contains links to all known minor railway web sites or web pages and these should display operating dates and times - be warned however, not all of these are as up to date as they should be! The books listed in the "Further Reading & Information" section may also give additional operating details. Additionally, for the majority of railways in the list, operating dates & times are available from the Compiler. This information is free, but not guaranteed! However, be aware that operation of many of the smaller gauge lines can be dependent on the whim of the operator, how many prospective passengers turn up or on the weather! Many lines have only one locomotive, so a failure can stop operation for the day or longer. If you turn up at a line that is not in operation - don't turn your back and walk away, check the rails for signs of recent use. Ask locals, you might get the answer that the operator always turns up at a certain time, or closes for lunch. Perhaps a local problem has caused operation to cease. See if the shed doors are open or unlocked. If the railway has been closed and/or lifted let the Compiler know! Don't be discouraged by the above, just plan your visits with care and an eye to the weather. Always try and check operating details if you are travelling a long way.

COMPILER'S NOTES

Welcome to the thirty-sixth edition of *MINOR RAILWAYS*. There are no major changes to report in this edition, beyond detailing the constantly changing minor railway scene with the usual selection of openings, closures and extensions. The growing interest in our smaller railways proves they are more than just tourist attractions or rides for children. Many of the railways have a fascinating and complex history and the diversity of motive power on show is truly amazing. It is true to say the range of railways covered in this book is so wide, that the only things they have in common are wheels running on two rails! An associated web site is available to support this book - **Minor Railways**. Details are given on page 2.

The list includes over 510 lines to visit and travel on. Information has been drawn from a wide range of sources and personal observation. My thanks are due to the many people who have kindly supplied information. This source of material is much appreciated and I welcome any news on new lines, closures or alterations so the list can be kept as up to date as possible. Any railway owners or operators reading this book, and finding their line missing or with incorrect information shown - please let me know! I would be especially pleased to hear of any new lines for inclusion.

Peter Scott - March 2024

SECTION 1
STANDARD GAUGE RAILWAYS

All **Standard Gauge Railways** giving rides to the general public are contained in this section; this includes demonstration lines giving short rides in steam centres and museums. Note that in Ireland standard gauge is 5' 3", as opposed to 4' 8½" elsewhere. The section is divided by geographical area: Channel Islands & Southern England, Midlands & Eastern England, Northern England, Wales, Scotland, Ireland.

The first passengers on a standard gauge preserved railway were carried on 18th June 1960, on the Middleton Railway in Leeds. This was a former industrial railway and the first ex-BR passenger line to see preservation was the Bluebell Railway, opened on 7th August 1960. Standard gauge preserved railways have come a long way from those small beginnings at Middleton and Sheffield Park. From there have grown a multitude of railways, steam centres and museums that now play a major part in the tourist industry of the British Isles. Total route mileage of these railways is now almost 350 miles.

Each entry has six columns associated with it:

Column 1   + NR/IE/NIR physical track connection exists.

Column 2   Route length of line in miles & chains, as available to passengers.
eg **7.13** is 7 miles 13 chains.

Column 3   Page number in relevant TRACKmaps book on which the line is shown.
Book number/Page number.

Column 4   Owning Company of line at grouping.
▲ Indicates the railway was built on a "greenfield" site.

Column 5   Ordnance Survey National Grid Reference. Reference refers to the main station or boarding point.

Column 6   Telephone number for enquires.
ⓘ Local Tourist Information Office. (e) Evenings only.

§   Private Railway. Access only available on advertised open days. Do not attempt to visit at other times. Please respect private property.

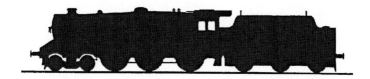

5

CHANNEL ISLANDS & SOUTHERN ENGLAND

Alderney Railway, Braye, Alderney
| | 2.00 | 5/17C | Admiralty | WA577081 | 07911 739572 |

Helston Railway, Prospidnick, Helston, Cornwall
| | 1.02 | 3/38G | GWR | SW645309 | 07901 977597 |

Bodmin Railway, Bodmin, Cornwall
| + | 6.14 | 3/9D | GWR | SX073664 | 01208 73555 |

Plym Valley Railway, Marsh Mills, Plymouth, Devon
| | 1.12 | 3/38C | GWR | SX521570 | 01752 345078 |

South Devon Railway, Buckfastleigh, Devon
| + | 6.55 | 3/8C | GWR | SX746663 | 01364 644370 |

Dartmouth Steam Railway, Paignton, Devon
| + | 6.57 | 3/8C | GWR | SX889606 | 01803 555872 |

Bideford Railway Heritage Centre, Bideford Station, Devon
| | 0.09 | | LSWR | SS457263 | 07854 590503 |

Tarka Valley Railway, Great Torrington, Devon
| | 0.12 | | LSWR | SS480198 | 07454 673809 |

Swanage Railway, Swanage, Dorset
| + | 5.47 | 5/20D | LSWR | SZ029789 | 01929 425800 |

Isle of Wight Steam Railway, Haven Street, Isle of Wight
| | 4.59 | 5/20D | IWCR | SZ556898 | 01983 882204 |

West Somerset Railway, Minehead, Somerset
| + | 19.51 | 3/7C&D | GWR | SS975463 | 01643 704996 |

Yeovil Railway Centre, Yeovil Junction Station, Somerset
| + | 0.25 | 5/36D | GWR | ST570141 | 01935 410420 |

Bristol Harbour Railway, Princes Wharf, Bristol
| | 1.10 | 3/6C | GWR | ST585723 | 0117 925 1470 |

Avon Valley Railway, Bitton, Gloucestershire
| | 2.35 | 3/17C | MR | ST670703 | 0117 932 5538 |

Somerset & Dorset Railway Heritage Trust, Midsomer Norton, Somerset
| | 0.74 | 3/13E | SDR | ST664536 | 01761 411221 |

East Somerset Railway, Cranmore, Somerset
| + | 1.63 | 3/13A | GWR | ST667430 | 01749 880417 |

Mid Hants Railway, Alresford, Hampshire
| + | 10.10 | 5/27D | LSWR | SU589324 | 01962 733810 |

Bluebell Railway, Sheffield Park, East Sussex
| + | 10.56 | 5/20B | LBSCR | TQ403237 | 01825 720800 |

Lavender Line, Isfield, Uckfield, East Sussex
| | 0.71 | 5/16B | LBSCR | TQ452171 | 01825 750515 |

Spa Valley Railway, Tunbridge Wells, Kent
| | 4.78 | 5/14B | LBSCR | TQ578384 | 01892 300141 |

Kent & East Sussex Railway, Tenterden, Kent
| | 10.10 | 5/20C | KESR | TQ882335 | 01580 765155 |

East Kent Railway, Shepherdswell, Kent
| | 2.08 | 5/10 | EKLR | TR258483 | 01304 832042 |

Dean Forest Railway, Norchard, Gloucestershire
| + | 4.45 | 3/21B | SWJR | SO629044 | 01594 845840 |

Swindon & Cricklade Railway, Blunsdon, Wiltshire
| | 2.20 | 3/38B | MSWJR | SU109898 | 01793 771615 |

Didcot Railway Centre, Didcot, Oxfordshire
Main Line
| + | 0.35 | 3/38A | GWR | SU526906 | 01235 817200 |

Branch Line
| + | 0.15 | 3/38A | GWR | SU523909 | 01235 817200 |

CHANNEL ISLANDS & SOUTHERN ENGLAND (Continued)

Cholsey & Wallingford Railway, Wallingford, Oxfordshire

2.28	3/4C	GWR	SU600891	01491 835067

Fawley Hill Railway, Henley-on-Thames, Buckinghamshire §

0.60		▲	SU756859	01491 574873

Fifield Railway, Windsor, Berkshire §

0.20		▲	SU907766	07831 485645

Chinnor & Princes Risborough Railway, Chinnor, Oxfordshire

+ 3.57	4/16B	GWR	SP757005	01844 353535

Buckinghamshire Railway Centre, Quainton Road, Buckinghamshire

Down Yard

0.34	4/15D	Met & GCR	SP738190	01296 655720

Up Yard

0.30	4/15D	Met & GCR	SP739190	01296 655720

MIDLANDS & EASTERN ENGLAND

Kingfisher Line, Titley Junction Station, Herefordshire §

0.52		GWR	SO328581	01544 340622

Great Welland Railway, Great Malvern, Worcestershire §

0.18		▲	SO804407	01531 890417

Gloucestershire Warwickshire Steam Railway, Toddington, Gloucestershire

13.75	3/15C	GWR	SP050323	01242 621405

Telford Steam Railway, Horsehay, Telford, Shropshire

0.61	4/22E	GWR	SJ675073	07816 762790

Severn Valley Railway, Bridgnorth, Shropshire

+ 16.01	4/23A	GWR	SO716926	01562 757900

Tyseley Locomotive Works, Tyseley, Birmingham, West Midlands

+ 0.15	4/19B	GWR	SP107841	0121 708 4960

Chasewater Railway, Brownhills, Staffordshire

1.57	4/22D	MR/Colliery	SK033072	01543 452623

Battlefield Line Railway, Shackerstone, Leicestershire

4.22	4/5C	LNW & MR	SK379065	01827 880754

Great Central Railway, Loughborough, Leicestershire

7.50	4/27C	GCR	SK543193	01509 632323

Mountsorrel Railway, Rothley, Leicestershire

1.02	4/27C	Quarry	SK570142	0116 237 4591

Northampton Ironstone Railway, Hunsbury Hill, Northampton, Northamptonshire

0.30	4/4F	Ironstone	SP735585	01604 702031

Northampton & Lamport Railway, Church Brampton, Northamptonshire

1.09	4/4E	LNWR	SP735667	01604 820327

Rushden, Higham & Wellingborough Railway, Rushden, Northamptonshire

0.30	4/9E	MR	SP957672	01933 353111

Rocks by Rail - The Living Ironstone Museum, Cottesmore, Rutland

0.40	4/10D	MR	SK886137	07974 171068

Cambrian Heritage Railways, Llynclys, Shropshire

0.62	3/31B	CamR	SJ284239	01691 728131

Cambrian Heritage Railways, Oswestry, Shropshire

1.35	3/31B	CamR	SJ294298	01691 728131

Crewe Heritage Centre, Crewe, Cheshire

+ 0.13	4/7B	LNWR	SJ709552	01270 212130

MIDLANDS & EASTERN ENGLAND (Continued)

Churnet Valley Railway, Cheddleton, Staffordshire
9.75	4/26B	NSR	SJ983520	01538 750755

Foxfield Railway, Blythe Bridge, Staffordshire
2.00	4/26A	Colliery	SJ958421	01782 396210

Ecclesbourne Valley Railway, Wirksworth, Derbyshire
Duffield Line
8.28	4/12A	MR	SK290541	01629 823076

Ravenstor Line
0.45	4/12A	MR	SK290541	01629 823076

Peak Rail, Matlock, Derbyshire
+	3.35	4/14E	MR	SK296602	07979 496488

Midland Railway - Butterley, Derbyshire
+	3.03	4/12A	MR	SK403519	01773 570140

Barrow Hill Roundhouse, Chesterfield, Derbyshire
+	0.34	2/28A	MR	SK413755	01246 472450

Great Central Railway (Nottingham), Ruddington, Nottinghamshire
+	9.08	4/27C	GCR/MOD	SK575322	0115 940 5705

Epping Ongar Railway, Chipping Ongar, Essex
5.67	2/4C	GER	TL551035	01277 365200

Mangapps Railway Museum, Burnham-on-Crouch, Essex
0.47	2/10C	▲	TQ943980	01621 784898

Colne Valley Railway, Castle Hedingham, Essex
0.49	2/4D	CVHR	TL773362	01787 461174

East Anglian Railway Museum, Chappel & Wakes Colne, Essex
+	0.26	2/4E	GER	TL898289	01206 242524

Nene Valley Railway, Wansford, Cambridgeshire
+	7.18	2/42D	LNWR	TL093980	01780 784444

Mid Suffolk Light Railway, Wetheringsett, Suffolk
0.21	2/12E	MSLR	TM129659	01449 766899

Long Shop Museum, Leiston, Suffolk
0.02		▲	TM443626	01728 832189

Bressingham Steam Museum, Bressingham, Diss, Norfolk
0.25	2/7F	▲	TM080806	01379 686900

Mid Norfolk Railway, East Dereham, Norfolk
+	12.79	2/13B	GER	TF997119	01362 851723

Lincolnshire Wolds Railway, Ludborough, Lincolnshire
1.50	2/27C	GNR	TF309960	01507 363881

Whitwell & Reepham Railway, Reepham, Norfolk
0.24	2/7E	MGNR	TG092216	01603 871694

North Norfolk Railway, Sheringham, Norfolk
+	5.10	2/8	MGNR	TG156431	01263 820800

NORTHERN ENGLAND

Ribble Steam Railway, Preston, Lancashire
+	1.57	4/30C	Prest Corp	SD504293	01772 728800

East Lancashire Railway, Bury, Greater Manchester
+	12.12	4/45A	LYR	SD802107	0161 764 7790

Keighley & Worth Valley Railway, Keighley, West Yorkshire
+	4.62	2/42B	MR	SE066413	01535 645214

Embsay & Bolton Abbey Steam Railway, Embsay, North Yorkshire
3.69	2/42C	MR	SE007533	01756 710614

NORTHERN ENGLAND (Continued)

Middleton Railway, Hunslet, Leeds, West Yorkshire

	0.70	2/36D	Colliery	SE305310	0113 271 0320

National Railway Museum, York, North Yorkshire

+	0.10	2/19	NER	SE593518	0844 815 3139

Derwent Valley Light Railway, Murton Park, York, North Yorkshire

	0.30	2/19B	DVLR	SE651523	01904 489966

Yorkshire Wolds Railway, Fimber, East Riding of Yorkshire

	0.24	2/19D	NER	SE911608	01377 338053

Lakeside & Haverthwaite Railway, Haverthwaite, Cumbria

	3.00	4/34D	FR	SD349843	01539 531594

Stainmore Railway, Kirkby Stephen, Cumbria

	0.19	4/36E	NER	NY769075	01768 371700

Eden Valley Railway, Warcop, Cumbria

+	2.24	4/36C	NER	NY753157	01768 342309

Wensleydale Railway, Leeming Bar, North Yorkshire

+	21.49	2/20D	NER	SE287901	01677 425805

Weardale Railway, Stanhope, Durham

+	15.77	2/44A	NER	NY998387	07719 757755

Locomotion: The National Railway Museum at Shildon, Durham

+	0.45	2/44D	NER	NZ240255	01388 777999

North Yorkshire Moors Railway, Grosmont, North Yorkshire

+	17.72	2/48D	NER	NZ828053	01751 472508

Tanfield Railway, Sunniside, Tyne & Wear

	2.50	2/44D	NER	NZ209585	07508 092365

Beamish - The Living Museum of the North, Stanley, Durham

Rowley Station

	0.20	2/42E	▲	NZ217550	0191 370 4000

Pockerley Waggonway

	0.15	2/42E	▲	NZ223544	0191 370 4000

Stephenson Steam Railway, North Shields, Tyne & Wear

	1.41	2/49A	NER/Colliery	NZ323691	0191 200 7146

Aln Valley Railway, Alnwick, Northumberland

	1.20	2/23D	NER	NU200121	0300 030 3311

WALES

Gwili Steam Railway, Bronwydd Arms, Carmarthen, Carmarthenshire

	4.00	3/38F	GWR	SN417239	01267 238213

Llanelli & Mynydd Mawr Railway, Cynheidre, Carmarthenshire

	0.30	3/38I	LMMR	SN493072	01554 759255

Barry Railway, Barry Island, Vale of Glamorgan

+	1.76	3/28B	BR	ST115667	07443 870136

Pontypool & Blaenavon Railway, Blaenavon, Torfaen

	2.28	3/26C	LNWR	SO234095	01495 707448

Llangollen & Corwen Railway, Llangollen, Denbighshire

	9.73	3/32D	GWR	SJ215422	01978 860979

SCOTLAND

Doon Valley Railway, Waterside, East Ayrshire
| + | 0.77 | 1/2C | Colliery | NS444082 | 01292 269260 |

Border Union Railway, Hawick, Scottish Borders
| | 0.34 | 1/25C | NBR | NT526002 | 07858 799261 |

Bo'ness & Kinneil Railway, Bo'ness, Falkirk
| + | 4.65 | 1/13 | NBR | NT004817 | 01506 822298 |

Scottish Vintage Bus Museum, Dunfermline, Fife
| | 0.18 | 1/25D | Navy | NT092918 | 07379 914801 |

Fife Heritage Railway, Leven, Fife
| | 0.32 | 1/15E | NBR | NO373007 | 01592 712815 |

Strathspey Railway, Aviemore, Highland
| + | 9.38 | 1/20D | HR | NH897127 | 01479 810725 |

Caledonian Railway, Brechin, Angus
| | 4.04 | 1/17E | CalR | NO602602 | 01356 622992 |

Royal Deeside Railway, Milton of Crathes, Aberdeenshire
| | 0.62 | 1/18F | GNSR | NO740962 | 01330 844416 |

Keith & Dufftown Railway, Dufftown, Moray
| | 10.14 | 1/19D | GNSR | NJ323414 | 01340 821181 |

IRELAND (5' 3" Gauge)

Downpatrick & County Down Railway, Downpatrick, Co Down
| | 1.26 | 6/20F | BCDR | J482442 | 028 4461 5779 |

Whitehead Railway Museum, Whitehead, Co Antrim
| + | 0.10 | 6/18D | NCC | J474923 | 028 2826 0803 |

SECTION 2
NARROW GAUGE & MINIATURE RAILWAYS

All **Narrow Gauge & Miniature Railways**, which are available to the general public, are included - provided they are a) 7¼" gauge or greater, b) ground level and c) permanent. Some private lines that are open to the public on a fairly regular basis have also been included, but please read the notes for column 5. The section is divided by country (ie Channel Islands & Isle of Man, England, Ireland, Scotland, Wales) and then by county/authority.

This section covers an amazing wide spectrum of railways. They range from lengthy lines such as the Romney, Hythe & Dymchurch, through lines in theme parks, garden centres, zoos, parks, or on the seafront; down to a small circle of track operated by a local Model Engineering Society. The very nature of the lines in this section means they can appear and disappear rapidly. This fact and their sheer variety, make them a fascinating subject to follow.

Each entry has six columns associated with it:

Column 1   Gauge in feet (') and inches ("). 7¼"/10¼" represents a dual gauge line.

Column 2   Layout. Where the layout is underlined, ie <u>E</u>, this indicates the line is laid (wholly or partly) on a former railway trackbed.

        E   End to End   D   Dumb-bell

        B   Balloon   or   C   Complex

        O   Circuit   or

Column 3   Route length of line in miles or yards, as available to passengers.

Column 4   Ordnance Survey National Grid Reference. Reference refers to the main station or boarding point.

Column 5   Additional Information.
- ♠   Separate entrance charge payable to gain access to railway.
- ✗   Entrance restricted to families only. No single or group adult admission.
- T   Operated to a published timetable.
- ♣   Limited operation (Less than one day a week, typically one or two Sundays a month).
- ♦   Operation on special events/occasions only.
- §   Private Railway. Access only available on advertised open days. Do not attempt to visit at other times. Please respect private property.
- Θ   Private Railway. Access available on advertised open days only with pre-booked ticket. Do not attempt to visit at other times. Please respect private property.

Column 6   Telephone number for enquires or operating dates & times.
                        ① Local Tourist Information Office. (e) Evenings only.

CHANNEL ISLANDS & ISLE OF MAN

ALDERNEY
Alderney Miniature Railway, Mannez Quarry
7¼"   O   400yds   WA601087   07911 739572

GUERNSEY
Sausmarez Manor Garden Railway, Sausmarez Road, St Martin
7¼"   O   350yds   WV329762   01481 235571

ISLE OF MAN
Crogga Valley Railway, Port Soderick
7¼"   E   450yds   SC335726   §   Open days
Great Laxey Mine Railway, Laxey
19"   E   390yds   SC433846   01624 861706
Groudle Glen Railway, Groudle Glen
2'   E   1,000yds   SC418786   01624 670453
Isle of Man Steam Railway, Douglas
3'   E   15¼ miles   SC377753   T   01624 662525
Manx Electric Railway, Derby Castle, Douglas
3'   E   17¾ miles   SC395774   T   01624 662525
Manx Steam & Model Engineering Club, Curraghs Wildlife Park, Ballaugh
5"/7¼"   C   1,000yds   SC367943   ♣   01624 897323
Snaefell Mountain Railway, Laxey
3' 6"   E   4¾ miles   SC433845   01624 662525

ENGLAND

BEDFORDSHIRE
Fancott Miniature Railway, The Fancott Public House, Fancott, Toddington
7¼"   C   400yds   TL022278   01525 872366
Great Whipsnade Railway, ZSL Whipsnade Zoo, Dunstable
2' 6"   O   1½ miles   TL005174   ♣   01582 872171
Great Woburn Railway, Woburn Safari Park, Woburn
20"   D   1,400yds   SP961342   ♣   01525 290407
Leighton Buzzard Railway, Page's Park, Leighton Buzzard
2'   E   3¼ miles   SP928242   T   01525 373888
Summerfields Miniature Railway, Rook Tree Farm, Haynes, Bedford
7¼"   C   850yds   TL099429   ♣   01234 743062

BERKSHIRE
Amnerfield Miniature Railway, Amner's Farm, Burghfield, Reading
5"/7¼"   D   930yds   SU680694   ♦   0118 983 3437
Ascot Locomotive Society, Ascot Racecourse, Winkfield Road, Ascot
3½"/5"7¼"   C   1,000yds   SU927693   ♣   Apr-Oct: 1st Sunday
Beale Park Railway, Beale Park, Lower Basildon, Pangbourne
10¼"   D   1,100yds   SU618782   ♣   0870 777 7160
Legoland Express, Legoland, Winkfield Road, Windsor
2'   O   500yds   SU939748   ♣   0871 222 2001
Pinewood (Wokingham) Miniature Railway, Pinewood Leisure Centre, Crowthorne
5"/7¼"   O   620yds   SU838661   ♣   07587 057885
Reading Model Engineers, Prospect Park, Bath Road, Reading
5"/7¼"   O   400yds   SU692724   ♣   01491 873393

BUCKINGHAMSHIRE
Bekonscot Light Railway, Model Village, Beaconsfield
| 7¼" | C | 191yds | SU939914 | ♠ | 01494 672919 |

Golding Spring Miniature Railway, Buckinghamshire Railway Centre, Quainton Road
| 5"/7¼" | O | 700yds | SP741189 | ♠ | 01296 655720 |

Lavendon Narrow Gauge Railway, Harrold Road, Lavendon
| 7¼" | C | 370yds | SP920535 | § | 01234 712653(e) |

Milton Keynes Light Railway, The Windmill, Caldecotte Lake, Milton Keynes
| 5"/7¼" | O | 250yds | SP887355 | | 07564 208003 |

CAMBRIDGESHIRE
Dunhams Wood Light Railway, Rodham Road, March
| 7¼" | B | 700yds | TL443975 | § | 01354 661997 |

Fenland Light Railway, Ramsey Mereside
| 7¼" | C | 350yds | TL300899 | ♣ | 01487 815628(e) |

Ferry Meadows Railway, Ferry Meadows Park, Ham Lane, Peterborough
| 10¼" | E | 700yds | TL148975 | | 07779 031764 |

Grantchester Woodland Railway, Fulbrooke Road, Cambridge
| 5"/7¼" | C | 880yds | TL434572 | ♣ | Apr-Oct: 2nd Sunday |

Riverside Miniature Railway, Riverside Park, St Neots
| 5"/7¼" | O | 340yds | TL179600 | | 01480 217037 |

CHESHIRE
Brookside Miniature Railway, Brookside Garden Centre, Poynton
| 7¼" | O | 950yds | SJ927852 | | 01625 872919 |

Crewe Heritage Centre Miniature Railway, Vernon Way, Crewe
| 7¼" | C | 600yds | SJ709553 | ♠ | 01270 212130 |

Eaton Park Railway, Eaton Hall, Eccleston, Chester
| 15" | B | 1½ miles | SJ414610 | ♠♦ | 01244 684400 |

Grosvenor Park Miniature Railway, Chester
| 7¼" | O | 340yds | SJ412663 | | 07530 397079 |

Gullivers World Railroad, Old Hall, Warrington
| 15" | O | 500yds | SJ590900 | ♠✗ | 01925 444888 |

Halton Miniature Railway, Town Park, Palacefields, Runcorn
| 7¼" | O | 1 mile | SJ548811 | | 01928 701965 |

Handforth Model Engineers, Meriton Road Park, Handforth
| 7¼" | O | 230yds | SJ856837 | | All year: Most Sundays |

High Legh Miniature Railway, High Legh Garden Centre, Knutsford
| 7¼" | O | 700yds | SJ700836 | | 01925 756991 |

Nantwich Methodist Church, Hospital Street, Nantwich
| 7¼" | E | 75yds | SJ651523 | | 01270 626340 |

Sandiway Miniature Railway, Blakemere Village, Northwich
| 7¼" | O | 500yds | SJ599703 | | All year: Sundays |

CORNWALL
Lappa Valley Steam Railway, St Newlyn East, Newquay
Main Line
| 15" | B | 1¼ miles | SW839573 | T | 01872 510317 |

Newlyn Branch Line
| 10¼" | E | 700yds | SW838558 | ♠ | 01872 510317 |

Woodland Railway
| 7¼" | O | 350yds | SW838558 | ♠ | 01872 510317 |

CORNWALL (Continued)

Launceston Steam Railway, Newport, Launceston
1' 11½"	E	2 miles	SX329850	T	01566 775665

Little Western Railway, Trenance Leisure Park, Newquay
7¼"	O	300yds	SW819614		01637 873342

Moseley Heritage Museum, Tumblydown Farm, Tolgus Mount, Redruth
2'	B	650yds	SW686428		01209 211191

North Cornwall Miniature Railway, St Teath, Bodmin
10¼"	C	760yds	SX048794	§	Open days (4 a year)

Paradise Railway, Paradise Park, Hayle
15"	O	240yds	SW554365	♠	01736 751020

Porterswick Junction Light Railway, Hidden Valley, Launceston
7¼"	O	800yds	SX278849	♠	01566 86463

CUMBRIA

Millerbeck Light Railway, Staveley-in-Cartmel, Newby Bridge
7¼"	C	750yds	SD378861	§	01539 530113

Ravenglass & Eskdale Railway, Ravenglass
15"	E	6¾ miles	SD086964	T	01229 717171

South Tynedale Railway, Alston
2'	E	4½ miles	NY717467	T	01434 382828

Threlkeld Quarry Railway, Mining Museum, Threlkeld, Keswick
2'	E	700yds	NY328244	01768 779747

DERBYSHIRE

Ashover Light Railway, Peak Rail, Rowsley
2'	E	280yds	SK261642	♦	07979 496488

Buxton Miniature Railway, Pavilion Gardens, Buxton
12¼"	O	320yds	SK055733	01298 23114

Chesterfield Model Engineers, St Peter & St Paul School, Hady, Chesterfield
5"/7¼"	C	600yds	SK397711	♣	07710 273614

Ecclesbourne Valley Railway, Wirksworth
Stone Line
2'	E	300yds	SK289542	01629 823076

Wirksworth Miniature Railway
7¼"	E	170yds	SK290540	01629 823076

Golden Valley Light Railway, Swanwick Junction, Midland Railway - Butterley
2'	E	1,400yds	SK415520	01773 570140

Hall Leys Miniature Railway, Hall Leys Park, Matlock
9½"	E	200yds	SK300600	07881 632405

Manor Park Miniature Railway, Manor Park Road, Glossop
7¼"	C	600yds	SK041945	07779 601180

Queens Park Miniature Railway, Boythorpe Road, Chesterfield
10¼"	O	530yds	SK379709	01246 345555

Steeple Grange Light Railway, Bolehill, Wirksworth
Killer's Branch
18"	E	780yds	SK288555	01629 55123(e)

Steeplehouse Quarry Branch
18"	E	150yds	SK288555	01629 55123(e)

DEVON

Beer Heights Light Railway, Pecorama, Underleys, Beer

| 7¼" | C | 1,300yds | SY224893 | ♠ | 01297 306007 |

Bickington Steam Railway, Trago Mills, Bickington

| 10¼" | B | 1¼ miles | SX821742 | | 01626 821111 |

Bicton Woodland Railway, Bicton Park Botanical Gardens, East Budleigh

| 18" | C | 1 mile | SY073860 | ♠ | 01395 568465 |

Devon Railway Centre, Cadeleigh Station, Bickleigh, Tiverton
Miniature Railway

| 7¼" | B | 450yds | SS938076 | | 01884 855671 |

Narrow Gauge Railway

| 2' | B | 360yds | SS938076 | | 01884 855671 |

Dino Express, Combe Martin Wildlife & Dinosaur Park, Combe Martin

| 15" | E | 400yds | SS600452 | ♠ | 01271 882486 |

Exeter & Teign Valley Railway, Christow Station, Doddiscombsleigh

| 2' | C | 244yds | SX839867 | § | 01647 253108 |

Exeter Model Engineers, St Katherines Priory, Polsloe Bridge, Exeter

| 5"/7¼" | E | 150yds | SX941938 | ♣ | 07788 577662 |

Kingsbridge & District Light Railway, The Quay, Kingsbridge

| 7¼" | E | 340yds | SX736440 | | 07885 227000 |

Lynton & Barnstaple Railway, Woody Bay, Martinhoe Cross, Lynton
Main Line

| 2' | E | 1,540yds | SS682464 | | 01598 763487 |

Miniature Railway

| 7¼" | E | 210yds | SS682464 | ♦ | 01598 763487 |

Milky Way Railway, The Milky Way Adventure Park, Clovelly

| 2' | O | 600yds | SS327229 | ♠ | 01237 431255 |

Morwellham Quay Mine Tramway, Morwellham, Tavistock

| 2' | C | 1,100yds | SX448699 | | 01822 832766 |

Otterton & East Budleigh Light Railway, Otterton, Budleigh Salterton

| 7¼" | C | 300yds | SY077851 | § | 01395 568955 |

Plymouth Miniature Steam, Goodwin Park, Pendeen Crescent, Southway, Plymouth

| 3½"/5"/7¼" | O | 800yds | SX491607 | ♣ | Apr-Oct: 1st & 3rd Sun |

South Devon Miniature Railway, South Devon Railway, Buckfastleigh

| 7¼" | O | 750yds | SX747663 | | 01364 644370 |

DORSET

Moors Valley Railway, Country Park, Ashley Heath, Ringwood

| 7¼" | C | 2,000yds | SU104060 | | 01425 471415 |

Poole Park Railway, Parkstone Road, Poole

| 10¼" | O | 660yds | SZ025912 | | 01202 123456 |

Rio Grande Railway, Lodmoor Country Park, Weymouth

| 10¼" | O | 550yds | SY685807 | | 01305 838000 |

Weymouth Model Engineers, Budmouth Technology College, Weymouth

| 5"/7¼" | O | 300yds | SY652792 | ♣ | All year: 1st & 3rd Sat |

DURHAM

Cleveland Model Engineers, Tees Cottage Pumping Station, Coniscliffe Road, Darlington

| 5"/7¼" | E | 250yds | NZ258139 | ♠♦ | Open days ① |

Teesside Small Gauge Railway, Preston Park, Eaglescliffe

| 5"/7¼" | O | 400yds | NZ429161 | ♣ | 01642 652675 |

Thorpe Light Railway, Whorlton, Barnard Castle

| 15" | D | 750yds | NZ107144 | ⊖ | 07833 194286 |

① 31 March/1 April, 18/19 May, 22/23 June, 14/15 September, 5/6 October

EAST RIDING OF YORKSHIRE
Hull Model Engineers, West Park, Kingston upon Hull
| 5"/7¼" | O | 445yds | TA075290 | | Apr-Sep: Sundays |

EAST SUSSEX
Alexandra Park Miniature Railway, Hastings
| 7¼" | O | 240yds | TQ807107 | | 07548 648793 |

Bentley Miniature Railway, Halland, Uckfield
| 7¼" | C | 1 mile | TQ484159 | | 0845 8672583 |

Drusillas Railway, Drusillas Park, Berwick, Alfriston
| 2' | O | 370yds | TQ525049 | ♠ | 01323 874100 |

Eastbourne Miniature Steam Railway, Lottbridge Drove, Eastbourne
| 7¼" | O | 880yds | TQ613012 | | 01323 520229 |

Hastings Miniature Railway, Rock-a-Nore Road, Hastings
| 10¼" | E | 600yds | TQ827094 | | 07789 725438 |

Paradise Park Railway, Tates Garden Centre, Avis Road, Newhaven
| 7¼" | O | 200yds | TQ448023 | | 01273 512123 |

Tinkers Park, Hadlow Down, Heathfield
Great Bush Railway
| 2' | E | 550yds | TQ538241 | ♠♣ | Open days ② |

Miniature Railway
| 7¼" | E | 80yds | TQ538241 | ♠♦ | Open days ② |

Volks Electric Railway, Madeira Drive, Seafront, Brighton
| 2' 8½" | E | 1 mile | TQ316038 | | 01273 292718 |

ESSEX
Audley End Miniature Railway, Audley End, Saffron Walden
| 10¼" | B | 1 mile | TL523379 | | 01799 510726 |

Barnards Miniature Railway, Barnards Farm Gardens, West Horndon
| 7¼" | C | 1,840yds | TQ634877 | ♠♣ | 01277 811262 |

Chappel Miniature Railway, East Anglian Railway Museum, Chappel & Wakes Colne
| 7¼" | E | 140yds | TL899288 | ♠ | 01206 242524 |

Chelmsford Miniature Railway, Meteor Way, Waterhouse Lane, Chelmsford
| 5"/7¼" | O | 330yds | TL699066 | | May-Sep: Sundays |

Colne Valley Miniature Railway, Castle Hedingham
| 7¼" | C | 400yds | TL773362 | ♠ | 01787 461174 |

Langford & Beeleigh Railway, Museum of Power, Langford, Maldon
| 7¼" | O | 400yds | TL836090 | ♠♣ | 01621 843183 |

Little Braxted Railway, Braxted Bakery, Witham
| 2' | O | 335yds | TL839140 | ♦ | 07740 117688 |

Maldon Promenade Petting Zoo Safari Railway, Promenade Park, Maldon
| 7¼" | O | 130yds | TL859065 | ♠ | 07487 547122 |

North Weald & District Miniature Railway, Harlow Garden Centre, Harlow
| 7¼" | C | 580yds | TL478067 | | 07583 084352 |

Poplar Miniature Railway, Poplar Nurseries, Marks Tey
| 7¼" | O | 350yds | TL898233 | | 01206 210374 |

② 1/2 June, 3/4 August, 28 September

ESSEX (Continued)

Royal Gunpowder Mills, Waltham Abbey
Bangs Galore & Gunpowder Creek Railway

7¼"	E	320yds	TL377011	♠	01992 707370

WARGM Railway

2' 6"	E	700yds	TL375013	♠♣	01992 707370

Southend Pier Railway, Southend

3'	E	2,026yds	TQ885849	T	01702 215620

Sutton Hall Railway, Rochford, Southend

10¼"	E	800yds	TQ889891	♣	01702 622057

Waterside Railway, Waterside Farm Sports Centre, Canvey Island

7¼"	C	1,000yds	TQ781849		Apr-Sep: Sundays

GLOUCESTERSHIRE

Bridge House Light Railway, Rectory Road, Frampton Cotterell

7¼"	O	400yds	ST665816	§	Bank Holiday Mondays

Cheltenham Model Engineers, Hatherley Lane, Cheltenham

5"/7¼"	O	216yds	SO913214	♣	07969 123334

GWR Museum Miniature Railway, Old Goods Shed, Coleford

7¼"	C	180yds	SO577105	♠	01594 833569

Perrygrove Railway, Perrygrove Farm, Coleford

15"	E	1,200yds	SO579095	01594 834991

Toddington Narrow Gauge Railway, Station Yard, Toddington

2'	E	600yds	SP049323	01242 234646

GREATER LONDON

Acton Miniature Railway, London Transport Museum Depot, Acton

7¼"	E	180yds	TQ194797	♠♦	020 7379 6344

Brockwell Park Miniature Railway, Brockwell Park, Herne Hill

7¼"	E	220yds	TQ318743	07973 613515

Chingford Model Engineers, Ridgeway Park, Chingford

5"/7¼"	C	480yds	TQ378937	♣	Apr-Sep: 3 Suns a month

Hampton & Kempton Waterworks Railway, Kempton Steam Museum, Hanworth

2'	O	315yds	TQ109709	01932 212235

Harrow & Wembley Model Engineers, Roxbourne Park, Eastcote

3½"/5"/7¼"	C	600yds	TQ118869	01923 779382

Holly Tree Railway, The Holly Tree Pub, Forest Gate

7¼"	O	75yds	TQ401860	020 8221 9830

Ilford & West Essex Model Engineers, Chadwell Heath Station

7¼"	C	300yds	TQ477877	♣	Apr-Sep: 1st Sunday

Lodge Farm Park Railway, Lodge Farm Park, Main Road, Romford

7¼"	D	600yds	TQ520893	♣	Apr-Oct: 2nd & 4th Suns

Mail Rail, Phoenix Place, Clerkenwell

2'	B	1,000yds	TQ310822	0300 0300 700

Royal Arsenal Narrow Gauge Railway, Crossness Engines, Abbey Wood

2'	E	428yds	TQ483811	♣	020 8311 3711

Ruislip Lido Railway, Reservoir Road, Ruislip

12"	B	1¼ miles	TQ089889	01895 622595

Sutton Model Engineers, Chatham Close, Sutton

5"/7¼"	O	176yds	TQ247665	♣	All year: 2nd Sunday

Waterworks Railway, London Museum of Water & Steam, Kew Bridge, Brentford

2'	E	150yds	TQ188781	♠	020 8568 4757

GREATER MANCHESTER

Dragon Miniature Railway, Marple Garden Centre, Marple

| 7¼" | D | 500yds | SJ937894 | | All year: WE. Sch Hol: Daily |

Haigh Railway, Haigh Woodland Park, Haigh, Wigan

| 15" | O | 1 mile | SD600083 | | 01942 832895 |

Lancashire Mining Museum, Astley Green, Tyldesley

| 2' | E | 300yds | SJ705999 | | 01942 895841 |

HAMPSHIRE

4 Kingdoms Adventure Park Railway, Headley, Newbury

| 10¼" | O | 450yds | SU509635 | ♠ | 01635 269678 |

Bankside Miniature Railway, Brambridge Park Garden Centre, Eastleigh

| 7¼" | E | 100yds | SU467222 | | 01962 713707 |

Brickworks Miniature Railway, Bursledon Brickworks Industrial Museum, Lower Swanwick

| 7¼" | D | 280yds | SU500098 | ♠♦ | 01489 576248 |

Burghclere Miniature Railway, Burghclere Sports Club, Burghclere

| 7¼" | O | 430yds | SU472612 | ♣ | 01635 278642 |

Eastleigh Lakeside Railway, Wide Lane, Eastleigh

| 7¼"/10¼" | O | 1¼ miles | SU449175 | | 023 8061 2020 |

Exbury Gardens Railway, Beaulieu

| 12¼" | C | 1¼ miles | SU423006 | ♠ | 023 8089 1203 |

Fareham Model Engineers, Titchfield, Fareham

| 7¼" | O | 310yds | SU541070 | ♦ | Open days: 27/28 July |

Hayling Light Railway, Seafront, Hayling Island

| 2' | E | 1 mile | SZ715988 | | 07902 446340 |

Hythe Pier Railway, Hythe

| 2' | E | 700yds | SU424081 | | 023 8084 0722 |

Paultons Railway, Paultons Park, Ower, Romsey

| 15" | O | 700yds | SU317167 | ♠ | 023 8081 4442 |

Ropley Miniature Railway, Ropley Station, Mid Hants Railway

| 10¼" | E | 370yds | SU629324 | | 01962 733810 |

Royal Victoria Railway, Royal Victoria Country Park, Netley

| 10¼" | O | 1,000yds | SU464079 | | 023 8045 6246 |

Southampton Model Engineers, Riverside Park, Bitterne Park, Southampton

| 7¼" | O | 360yds | SU437144 | | Apr-Sep: Sundays |

Wellington Country Park Railway, Riseley

| 12¼" | O | 500yds | SU730627 | ♠ | 0118 932 6444 |

HEREFORDSHIRE

Alan Keef Limited, Lea Line, Ross-on-Wye

| 2' | E | 200yds | SO665214 | § | Open day: 28 September |

Broomy Hill Railway, Herefordshire Waterworks Museum, Hereford

| 5"/7¼" | C | 750yds | SO496392 | ♣ | Apr-Sep: 2nd & Last Sun |

HERTFORDSHIRE

East Herts Miniature Railway, Van Hage Garden Centre, Great Amwell

| 7¼" | C | 580yds | TL367124 | | 01920 870811 |

North London Model Engineers, Colney Heath, Hatfield

| 5"/7¼" | C | 900yds | TL197057 | ♣ | May-Oct: 1st & 3rd Sun |

Rex Express, Hertfordshire Zoo, Broxbourne

| 10¼" | O | 300yds | TL338068 | ♠ | 01992 470490 |

Vanstone Woodland Railway, Vanstone Park Garden Centre, Codicote

| 10¼" | B | 560yds | TL213200 | | 01438 820412 |

Watford Miniature Railway, Cassiobury Park, Watford

| 10¼" | C | 600yds | TQ090972 | | All year: WE. Sch Hol: Daily |

ISLE OF WIGHT
Isle of Wight Model Engineers, Northwood Recreation Ground, Cowes
| 5"/7¼" | O | 180yds | SZ488952 | ♣ | 07707 674225 |

KENT
Bredgar & Wormshill Light Railway, Bredgar, Sittingbourne
| 2' | E | 700yds | TQ873585 | ♣ | 01622 884254 |

Elham Valley Line Trust, Peene, Folkestone
| 7¼" | C | 100yds | TR185378 | ♠ | 01303 273014 |

Faversham Miniature Railway, Brogdale Farm, Faversham
| 9" | C | 900yds | TR006596 | | 01795 474211 |

Knees Woodland Miniature Railway, East Kent Railway, Shepherdswell
| 7¼" | C | 260yds | TR258484 | | 01304 832042 |

Richmond Light Railway, Richmond Farm, Hawkenbury
| 2' | C | 730yds | TQ809462 | ☉ | Open day: 10 August |

Romney, Hythe & Dymchurch Railway, Hythe
| 15" | B | 14 miles | TR153347 | T | 01797 362353 |

Sittingbourne & Kemsley Light Railway, Sittingbourne
| 2' 6" | E | 1¾ miles | TQ904642 | T | 01795 424899 |

Strand Park Miniature Railway, Strand Leisure Park, Pier Road, Gillingham
| 7¼" | O | 400yds | TQ785693 | | 01634 852907 |

Swanley New Barn Railway, Swanley Park, Swanley
| 7¼" | B | 900yds | TQ515696 | | 01322 380936 |

LANCASHIRE
Burnley & Pendle MRS, Thompson Park, Burnley
| 7¼" | C | 1,000yds | SD844333 | | 07957 714148 |

Happy Mount Park Express, Happy Mount Park, Bare, Morecambe
| 10¼" | O | 200yds | SD456653 | | 01524 401140 |

Lancaster & Morecambe Model Engineers, Cinderbarrow, Burton-in-Kendal
| 5"/7¼" | O | 400yds | SD513758 | | 01524 781767 |

Leyland Model Engineers, Worden Park, Leyland
| 7¼" | O | 900yds | SD538209 | | 01772 455580 |

Pleasure Beach Express, Ocean Boulevard, South Shore, Blackpool
| 21" | O | 1,000yds | SD306333 | ♠ | 0871 222 1234 |

St Annes Miniature Railway, Seafront, St Annes
| 10¼" | O | 680yds | SD322282 | | 01772 547431 |

West Lancashire Light Railway, Hesketh Bank, Preston
| 2' | E | 300yds | SD448229 | | 01772 815881 |

Windmill Farm Railway, Red Cat Lane, Burscough Bridge
| 15" | E | 750yds | SD427156 | ♠ | 01704 892282 |

LEICESTERSHIRE
Abbey Pumping Station Railway, Corporation Road, Leicester
| 2' | E | 300yds | SK589067 | ♣ | 0116 299 5111 |

Conkers Railway, Conkers, Moira
| 2' | D | 400yds | SK309158 | ♠ | 01283 216633 |

Iron Moose Express, Twinlakes Park, Melton Mowbray
| 15" | B | 1,000yds | SK772213 | ♠✘ | 01664 567777 |

Leicester Model Engineers, Abbey Park, Leicester
| 5"/7¼" | O | 750yds | SK584055 | | 07758 620283 |

LEICESTERSHIRE (Continued)

Melton Mowbray Miniature Railway, Wilton Park, Leicester Road, Melton Mowbray

10¼"	O	480yds	SK750190		07565 690125

Quarry Bottom Railway, Mountsorrel & Rothley Community Heritage Centre, Rothley

2'	O	140yds	SK569142	♣	0116 237 4591

Stapleford Miniature Railway, Stapleford Park, Melton Mowbray

10¼"	B	1¼ miles	SK812183	♦	Open days ③

LINCOLNSHIRE

Belton House Miniature Railway, Belton, Grantham

7¼"	D	570yds	SK927394	♣	01476 566116

Cleethorpes Coast Light Railway, Seafront, Cleethorpes

15"	E	1¼ miles	TA315078	T	01472 604657

Crowle Peatland Railway, Dole Road, Crowle

3'	E	510yds	SE757141	♣	07739 921835

Evergreens Miniature Railway, Dawn Bank, Keal Cotes, Spilsby

7¼"	C	417yds	TF369606	♣	Easter-Oct: Last Saturday

Grimsby & Cleethorpes Model Engineers, Waltham Windmill, Grimsby

5"/7¼"	C	500yds	TA259034		Apr-Oct: Sundays

Kirkby Green Light Railway, Scopwick, Metheringham

10¼"	C	1,600yds	TF090580	§	Open days ④

Lincoln Model Engineers, Sports Ground, North Scarle, Lincoln

5"/7¼"	O	600yds	SK852668	♣	01522 881760

Lincolnshire Coast Light Railway, Skegness Water Leisure Park, Skegness

2'	E	800yds	TF562671		01754 899400

Mablethorpe Miniature Railway, Queens Park, Mablethorpe

7¼"	O	200yds	TF510847		01507 474939 ①

North Ings Farm Narrow Gauge Railway, Dorrington, Sleaford

2'	O	400yds	TF098527	♣	01526 833100

Ropsley Heath Light Railway, Chain Lane, Ropsley, Grantham

10¼"	O	580yds	SK998355	§	07966 333090

Southfield Light Railway, Louth

7¼"	C	1¼ miles	TF336859	§	07720 091111

Springy's Railroad, Adventure Land, Springfields, Spalding

7¼"	O	180yds	TF265240		01775 723909

MERSEYSIDE

Equatorial Express, Knowsley Safari Park, Prescot, St Helens

15"	D	780yds	SJ460936	♣	0151 430 9009

Merseyside LS & ME, Harthill Road, Allerton, Liverpool

5"/7¼"	O	130yds	SJ402876		All year: Sundays

Pleasureland Miniature Railway, South Marine Park, Southport

15"	E	750yds	SD330174		01704 531957

Royden Park Miniature Railway, Frankby, West Kirby

7¼"	C	800yds	SJ247858		All year: Sundays

Whitfield Light Railway, The Hayloft, Sandy Lane Farm, Widnes

10¼"	E	300yds	SJ550884		07852 186328

③ 8/9 June, 24-26 August
④ Apr-Sep: Last Sunday or Bank Holiday Monday

NORFOLK

Barton House Riverside Railway, Hartwell Road, Wroxham
| 7¼" | E | 167yds | TG304177 | § | 01603 782470 |

Brandon Model Engineers, Fengate Farm, Weeting, Brandon
| 3½"/5"/7¼" | O | 400yds | TL770886 | ♠♦ | Open days: 19-21 July |

Bressingham Steam Museum, Diss
Fen Railway
| 1' 11½" | O | 1¼ miles | TM080806 | ♠ | 01379 686900 |

Garden Railway
| 10¼" | B | 680yds | TM080807 | ♠ | 01379 686900 |

Miniature Railway
| 5"/7¼" | O | 200yds | TM080806 | ♠♦ | 01379 686900 |

Waveney Valley Railway
| 15" | O | 1½ miles | TM080805 | ♠ | 01379 686900 |

Bure Valley Railway, Wroxham
| 15" | E | 8¾ miles | TG303187 | T | 01263 733858 |

Langley School Miniature Railway, Loddon
| 7¼" | E | 200yds | TG353006 | § | School open day |

Lynnsport Miniature Railway, Lynnsport Leisure Centre, Kings Lynn
| 5"/7¼" | O | 230yds | TF633209 | | 01553 764245(e) |

Norton Hill Light Railway, Hall Farm, Snettisham
| 7¼" | B | 600yds | TF688345 | § | Open days ⑤ |

Norwich Model Engineers, Eaton Park, South Park Avenue, Norwich
| 5"/7¼" | O | 900yds | TG208075 | ♣ | 01379 740578 |

Pettitts Animal Adventure Park Miniature Railway, Reedham
| 10¼" | O | 480yds | TG425025 | ♠✖ | 01493 700094 |

Strumpshaw Hall Steam Museum Railway, Brundall
| 2' | O | 680yds | TG347065 | ♠ | 01603 714535 |

Top Field Light Railway, Whitwell & Reepham Railway, Reepham
| 7¼" | E | 170yds | TG092216 | ♣ | 01603 871694 |

Wells & Walsingham Light Railway, Wells-Next-The-Sea
| 10¼" | E | 4 miles | TF925430 | T | 01328 711630 |

NORTHAMPTONSHIRE

Billing Aquadrome Railway, Northampton
| 15" | O | 1,000yds | SP810614 | | 01604 408181 |

Northampton Model Engineers, Lower Delapre Park, Northampton
| 5"/7¼" | B | 650yds | SP756593 | ♣ | 07907 051388 |

Wicksteed Park Railway, Kettering
| 2' | O | 1¼ miles | SP881771 | | 01536 512475 |

NORTHUMBERLAND

Aln Valley Miniature Railway, Aln Valley Railway, Alnwick
| 7¼" | E | 165yds | NU200121 | | 0300 030 3311 |

Heatherslaw Light Railway, Heatherslaw Mill, Ford, Coldstream
| 15" | E | 1¾ miles | NT934384 | T | 01890 820244 |

NORTH YORKSHIRE

Cedarbarn Miniature Railway, Thornton Road, Pickering
| 7¼" | D | 430yds | SE815832 | | 01751 475614 |

Chainbridge Miniature Railway, The Carrs, Ruswarp
| 7¼" | O | 700yds | NZ885088 | | 01947 600109 |

⑤ Three weekends in July & August

NORTH YORKSHIRE (Continued)

Daktari Express, Flamingo Land, Kirby Misperton, Malton
2'	O	1,900yds	SE778800	♠	0800 408 8840

Hambleton Valley Miniature Railway, Bolton Abbey Station, Embsay & Bolton Abbey Railway
7¼"	E	125yds	SE061534	01756 710614

Lightwater Express, Lightwater Valley, North Stainley, Ripon
15"	O	1,300yds	SE284758	♠	01765 635321

Moorland Railway, Staintondale, Scarborough
7¼"	D	500yds	SE975996	§	07771 886855

National Railway Museum, Leeman Road, York
7¼"	C	790yds	SE593519	0844 815 3139

Newby Hall Railway, Skelton on Ure, Ripon
10¼"	D	1,000yds	SE349672	♠	01423 322583

North Bay Railway, Northstead Manor Gardens, Scarborough
20"	E	1,300yds	TA035898	01723 368791

Ryedale Miniature Railway, Pottergate, Gilling East
3½"/5"/7¼"	O	400yds	SE613770	Apr-Sep: Sundays

Saltburn Miniature Railway, Valley Gardens, Saltburn
15"	E	715yds	NZ668215	07813 153975

Wolds Way Lavender Railway, Wintringham, Malton
7¼"	B	350yds	SE874744	♠	01944 758641

York Model Engineers, Dringhouses, York
5"/7¼"	O	530yds	SE585502	♣	May-Sep: Last Sun

NOTTINGHAMSHIRE

Chesterfield Model Engineers, Papplewick Pumping Station, Ravenshead
5"/7¼"	O	260yds	SK582521	♠♦	0115 963 2938

Nottingham Model Engineers, Nottingham Heritage Centre, Ruddington
7¼"	O	1,000yds	SK574322	♠	0115 940 5705

Sherwood Forest Railway, Edwinstowe, Mansfield
15"	E	550yds	SK586655	01623 515339

OXFORDSHIRE

Blenheim Park Railway, Blenheim Palace, Woodstock
15"	E	1,000yds	SP443162	♠	01993 810530

Cotswold Wildlife Park Railway, Burford
2'	O	1,500yds	SP239084	♠	01993 823006

Cutteslowe Park Miniature Railway, Cutteslowe, Oxford
5"/7¼"	C	500yds	SP510106	♣	01367 700550

RUTLAND

Melton Mowbray Model Engineers, Sports Club, Whissendine
5"/7¼"	O	400yds	SK820142	♣	Apr-Sep: 3rd Sunday

SHROPSHIRE

Mine Railway, Blists Hill Victorian Town, Madeley, Telford
2'	E	235yds	SJ694032	♠	01952 433424

Woodseaves Miniature Railway, Woodseaves Garden Plants Nursery, Market Drayton
7¼"	C	430yds	SJ687305	01630 653161

SOMERSET

Ashton Park Railway, Ashton Court Park, Bristol
| 5"/7¼" | O | 530yds | ST554729 | ♣ | 0117 963 9174 |

Bath & West Railway, Royal Bath & West Showground, Shepton Mallet
| 5"/7¼" | O | 800yds | ST633396 | ♣♦ | 01749 870662(e) |

East Somerset Miniature Railway, East Somerset Railway, Cranmore
| 7¼" | E | 400yds | ST667430 | ♦ | 01749 880417 |

Gartell Light Railway, Common Lane, Yenston, Templecombe
| 2' | C | 1,350yds | ST718218 | § | 01963 370752 |

Isle Abbots Railway, Isle Abbotts, Ilminster
| 7¼" | C | 1,200yds | ST352208 | § | Open days ⑥ |

Puxton Park Railway, Hewish, Weston-super-Mare
| 10¼" | O | 400yds | ST395629 | ♣✗ | 01934 523500 |

Strawberry Line Miniature Railway, Avon Valley Adventure & Wildlife Park, Keynsham
| 7¼" | O | 325yds | ST670688 | ♣♣ | 0117 986 4929 |

Westonzoyland Light Railway, Westonzoyland Pumping Station, Bridgwater
| 2' | E | 150yds | ST340328 | ♦ | 01278 691595 |

SOUTH YORKSHIRE

Abbeydale Miniature Railway, Abbeydale Road South, Dore
| 5"/7¼" | C | 750yds | SK322816 | ♣ | Apr-Oct: Alternate Sundays |

Rotherham Model Engineers, Rosehill Victoria Park, Rawmarsh, Rotherham
| 7¼" | C | 300yds | SK438973 | | 01709 543788 |

Rother Valley Railway, Rother Valley Country Park, Killamarsh
| 7¼" | D | 800yds | SK453828 | | 0114 247 1452 |

Thorne Park Railway, Thorne
| 5"/7¼" | O | 400yds | SE687130 | | Apr-Sep: Sundays |

Wortley Forge Miniature Railway, Thurgoland, Stocksbridge
| 5"/7¼" | O | 500yds | SK295999 | | 0114 288 7576 |

STAFFORDSHIRE

Amerton Railway, Amerton Farm & Craft Centre, Weston, Stafford
| 2' | O | 1,400yds | SJ994278 | | 01889 271337 |

Apedale Valley Light Railway, Apedale Country Park, Newcastle-under-Lyme
| 2' | E | 500yds | SJ823484 | | 0845 094 1953 |

Baggeridge Miniature Railway, Baggeridge Country Park, Wombourne
| 5"/7¼" | C | 580yds | SO898930 | ♣ | 01902 882605 |

Chasewater Narrow Gauge Railway, Chasewater Railway, Brownhills
| 2' | E | 170yds | SK033072 | ♦ | 01543 452623 |

Drayton Manor Park, Fazeley, Tamworth
Polperro Express Railway
| 2' | O | 1,000yds | SK194016 | ♣ | 0844 472 1950 |

Thomas Land Railway
| 2' | E | 550yds | SK195017 | ♣ | 0844 472 1950 |

Foxfield Miniature Railway, Foxfield Railway, Blythe Bridge
| 7¼" | B | 350yds | SJ958421 | | 01782 396210 |

Hilcote Valley Railway, Fletchers Country Garden Centre, Eccleshall
| 7¼" | O | 500yds | SJ842292 | | 01785 851057 |

⑥ As advertised at www.isle-abbotts.org.uk

STAFFORDSHIRE (Continued)

Leek & Rudyard Railway, Rudyard, Leek
| 10¼" | E | 1¼ miles | SJ956579 | | 01538 269948 |

Little Hay Miniature Railway, Balleny Green, Little Hay, Shenstone
| 5"/7¼" | C | 700yds | SK122027 | ♦ | All year: 1st Sunday |

Riverside Miniature Railway, Meadow Road, Burton upon Trent
| 7¼" | O | 285yds | SK255235 | ♣ | Apr-Oct: 3rd Sunday |

Stafford Model Engineers, County Agricultural Show Ground, Stafford
| 5"/7¼" | C | 590yds | SJ957256 | ♦ | Certain events at Show Ground |

Statfold Barn Railway, Tamworth
Field Railway
| 2' | B | 1 mile | SK241064 | ♠ | 01827 830389 |

Mease Valley Light Railway
| 12¼" | E | 880yds | SK241064 | ♠ | 01827 830389 |

Trentham Fern Miniature Railway, Trentham, Stoke-on-Trent
| 7¼" | B | 800yds | SJ867404 | ♠ | 01782 646646 |

Weston Park Railway, Weston-under-Lizard, Shifnal
| 7¼" | D | 1,450yds | SJ808106 | ♠ | 01952 852100 |

SUFFOLK

Blyth Valley Light Railway, Steamworks, Southwold
| 7¼" | O | 165yds | TM499765 | | 01502 725422 |

East Suffolk Light Railway, Carlton Colville, Lowestoft
| 2' | E | 350yds | TM506902 | ♠ | 01502 518459 |

Pleasurewood Hills Theme Park, Corton, Lowestoft
Big Train
| 2' | O | 1,100yds | TM543966 | ♠ | 01502 586000 |

Miniature Railway
| 7¼" | O | 1,100yds | TM543966 | ♠ | 01502 586000 |

SURREY

Frimley Lodge Miniature Railway, Frimley Lodge Park, Frimley
| 3½"/5"/7¼" | O | 1,000yds | SU891560 | ♣ | 07710 606461 |

Great Cockcrow Railway, Hardwick Lane, Lyne, Chertsey
| 7¼" | C | 2,000yds | TQ027662 | | 01932 565474 |

Guildford Model Engineers, Stoke Park, Guildford
| 7¼" | O | 334yds | TQ009508 | ♣ | Mar-Oct: 3rd Sunday |

Mizens Railway, Barrs Lane, Knaphill, Woking
| 7¼" | C | 1,500yds | SU967595 | | 020 8890 1978 |

Old Kiln Light Railway, Rural Life Living Museum, Tilford, Farnham
| 2' | E | 600yds | SU859434 | ♠ | 01252 795571 |

Surrey Model Engineers, Mill Lane, Leatherhead
| 5"/7¼" | C | 900yds | TQ161563 | ♣ | 020 8397 3932 |

Thames Ditton Miniature Railway, Claygate Lane, Thames Ditton
| 7¼" | C | 680yds | TQ162662 | ♣ | 020 8398 3985 |

TYNE & WEAR
Lakeshore Railroad, South Marine Park, South Shields
9½"	O	555yds	NZ373675		07745 350983

Tyneside Model Engineers, Exhibition Park, Newcastle
5"/7¼"	O	217yds	NZ246659	♣	01670 816072(e)

WARWICKSHIRE
Avonvale Miniature Railway, Hillers Farm Shop, Dunnington, Alcester
5"/7¼"	O	600yds	SP067539	♣	01789 773057

Bridge View Light Railway, Russells Garden Centre, Baginton
7¼"	O	300yds	SP337752	♣	024 7699 1441

Echills Wood Railway, Kingsbury Water Park, Bodymoor Heath
7¼"	O	1,500yds	SP205960		01926 498705(e)

Rainsbrook Valley Railway, Onley Lane, Rugby
7¼"	O	1,680yds	SP513727	♣	01604 740529(e)

WEST MIDLANDS
GEC (Coventry) Model Engineers, Copsewood Sports Ground, Allard Way, Coventry
7¼"	C	350yds	SP367781	♣	May-Oct: 1st Sunday

WEST SUSSEX
Amberley Museum Railway, Amberley, Arundel
2'	E	880yds	TQ028121	♠	01798 831370

Chichester Model Engineers, Bognor Road, Chichester
7¼"/10¼"	O	245yds	SU871047	♣	Apr-Sep: 3rd Sunday

Hollycombe Steam in the Country, Liphook
Garden Railway
7¼"	O	400yds	SU854294	♠	01428 724900

Quarry Railway
2'	B	1,400yds	SU854294	♠	01428 724900

Hotham Park Miniature Railway, Bognor Regis
12¼"	O	900yds	SZ939995		01638 669123

Ingfield Light Railway, Ingfield Manor School, Five Oaks, Billingshurst
10¼"	C	900yds	TQ091287	§	Open days ⑦

Littlehampton Miniature Railway, Mewsbrook Park, Littlehampton
12¼"	E	800yds	TQ042016		01903 719876

South Downs Light Railway, Pulborough Garden Centre, Pulborough
10¼"	O	1,100yds	TQ033183		07518 753784

Stansted Park Light Railway, Stansted Park, Rowland's Castle
7¼"	O	850yds	SU759100		023 9241 3324

WEST YORKSHIRE
Bradford Model Engineers, Northcliffe Woods, Shipley
5"/7¼"	O	550yds	SE142366		Apr-Sep: Sundays

Brighouse & Halifax Model Engineers, Cawcliffe Road, Brighouse
7¼"	C	450yds	SE143239	♣	Apr-Oct: 2nd Sunday

Clayton Flyer Miniature Railway, Whistlestop Valley, Clayton West
7¼"	O	300yds	SE259112		01484 865727

Greenhead Park Miniature Railway, Huddersfield
5"/7¼"	O	590yds	SE134170		07930 330450

⑦ As advertised at www.ingfieldlightrailway.co.uk

WEST YORKSHIRE (Continued)

Kirklees Light Railway, Whistlestop Valley, Clayton West

| 15" | E | 3¼ miles | SE259112 | T | 01484 865727 |

National Coal Mining Museum, New Road, Overton, Wakefield

| 2' 6" | E | 480yds | SE253165 | | 01924 848806 |

Pugneys Light Railway, Pugneys Country Park, Wakefield

| 7¼" | B | 740yds | SE324179 | | 01924 302360 |

Royds Park Miniature Railway, Cleckheaton

| 5"/7¼" | O | 170yds | SE200248 | | 07928 337668 |

Shibden Miniature Railway, Shibden Park, Stump Cross, Halifax

| 10¼" | O | 750yds | SE109261 | | 07854 658635 |

Thornes Park Railway, Lawefield Lane, Wakefield

| 7¼" | O | 800yds | SE323201 | | 01924 302382 |

West Riding Small Locomotive Society, Bradford Road, Tingley, Morley

| 7¼" | O | 240yds | SE291261 | | 0113 238 0355 |

WILTSHIRE

Coate Water Miniature Railway, Coate Water Country Park, Swindon

| 5"/7¼" | C | 1,400yds | SU179827 | | All year: Sundays |

Longleat Railway, Longleat House, Warminster

| 15" | B | 1 mile | ST808432 | ♠ | 01985 845408 |

Waterside Miniature Railway, Blunsdon Station, Swindon & Cricklade Railway

| 7¼" | E | 85yds | SU110897 | | 01793 771615 |

WORCESTERSHIRE

Coalyard Miniature Railway, Severn Valley Railway, Kidderminster Town Station

| 7¼" | E | 430yds | SO837762 | | 01562 757900 |

Cropthorne Light Railway, Cropthorne, Evesham

| 10¼" | E | 380yds | SP003449 | § | May Day BH: Sun & Mon |

Evesham Vale Light Railway, The Valley, Evesham

| 15" | B | 1,200yds | SP044465 | | 01386 422282 |

Worcester Model Engineers, Waverley Street, Cherry Orchard, Worcester

| 3½"/5"/7¼" | O | 400yds | SO852533 | ♣ | Apr-Sep: 3rd Sunday |

Wythall Miniature Railway, The Transport Museum, Wythall

| 3½"/5"/7¼" | O | 300yds | SP072750 | ♠♦ | 01564 826471 |

IRELAND

COUNTY ANTRIM

Carnfunnock Family Fun Zone, Carnfunnock Country Park, Larne

| 7¼" | D | 490yds | D384067 | | 028 2858 3269 |

Giant's Causeway & Bushmills Railway, Bushmills

| 3' | E | 2 miles | C943437 | T | 028 2073 2844 |

COUNTY DONEGAL

Difflin Lake Railway, Oakfield Park, Raphoe

| 15" | C | 2 miles | C274033 | § | 00 353 7491 73068 |

Fintown Railway, Fintown

| 3' | E | 2¼ miles | B924022 | | 00 353 7495 46280 |

COUNTY DOWN
Delamont Miniature Railway, Delamont Country Park, Mullagh, Killyleagh
| 10¼" | O | 1,000yds | J510508 | | 028 4482 8333 |
Drumawhey Junction Railway, Upper Gransha Road, Donaghadee
| 7¼" | C | 1,300yds | J547761 | ♣ | 028 9145 3563 |
Pickie Family Fun Park Railway, Seafront, Bangor
| 7¼" | B | 400yds | J501820 | | 028 9145 0746 |

COUNTY GALWAY
Leisureland Express, Seafront, Salthill, Galway
| 2' | O | 350yds | M277236 | | 00 353 91 521455 |

COUNTY LAOIS
Stradbally Woodland Railway, Stradbally Hall, Stradbally
| 3' | B | 880yds | S567965 | ♦ | 00 353 502 25444 |

COUNTY LEITRIM
Cavan & Leitrim Railway, Dromod
| 3' | E | 400yds | N055900 | | 00 353 71 9638599 |

COUNTY LONDONDERRY
Damhead Miniature Railway, Turnakibbock, Damhead, Coleraine
| 7¼" | C | 600yds | C895303 | ♣ | 028 7034 4723 ⓘ |

COUNTY MAYO
Bog Train, Mayo North Heritage Centre, Enniscoe, Crossmolina
| 3' | E | 400yds | G143143 | ♦ | 00 353 96 31809 |
Westport House Express, Westport
| 15" | B | 700yds | L987846 | ♠ | 00 353 98 27766 |

COUNTY MEATH
Steam Train Express, Emerald Park, Curragha, Ashbourne
| 2' | O | 490yds | O020560 | ♠ | 00 353 1 835 1999 |

COUNTY WATERFORD
Tramore Miniature Railway, Leisure Park, Seafront, Tramore
| 15" | O | 400yds | S585012 | | 00 353 51 381572 ⓘ |
Waterford & Suir Valley Railway, Kilmeadan, Waterford
| 3' | E | 4¾ miles | S515108 | T | 00 353 51 384058 |

SCOTLAND

ABERDEENSHIRE
Alford Valley Community Railway, Old Station, Alford
| 2' | E | 1,500yds | NJ580159 | | |

DUMFRIES & GALLOWAY
Agnew Park Miniature Railway, Seafront, Stranraer
| 7¼" | O | 810yds | NX055612 | | 01776 703535 |

EAST LOTHIAN
East Links Family Park Railway, West Barns, Dunbar
| 2' | O | 1,000yds | NT649787 | ♠ | 01368 863607 |

FIFE
Craigtoun Miniature Railway, Craigtoun Country Park, St Andrews
15"	O	400yds	NO482141		01334 472013

Kirkcaldy Model Engineers, Beveridge Park, Kirkcaldy
5"/7¼"	O	570yds	NT269911	♣	Apr-Sep: 2nd Sunday

West of Fife Munitions Railway, Scottish Vintage Bus Museum, Dunfermline
2'	E	280yds	NT092919	♣	07379 914801

HIGHLAND
Ness Islands Railway, Whin Island, Bught Park, Inverness
7¼"	D	870yds	NH658434	01463 243132

MIDLOTHIAN
Vogrie Park Miniature Railway, Vogrie Country Park, Newtongrange
7¼"	O	485yds	NT377631	07754 441211

NORTH LANARKSHIRE
Kirkintilloch Model Engineers, Colzium Lennox Estate, Kilsyth
3½"/5"/7¼"	O	220yds	NS730786	♣	0141 776 5421(e)

PERTH & KINROSS
Wester Pickston Railway, Glenalmond, Methven, Perth
5"/7¼"	C	1,500yds	NN984283	♦	Open days ⑧

SCOTTISH BORDERS
Ayton Castle Railway, Eyemouth
10¼"	B	300yds	NT928614	01890 781612

SOUTH AYRSHIRE
Tam O'Shanter Express, Heads of Ayr Farm Park, Ayr
10¼"	O	500yds	NS298180	♠	01292 441210

SOUTH LANARKSHIRE
Clyde Valley Express, Clyde Valley Family Park, Crossford, Carluke
2'	O	1,000yds	NS831461	01555 861222

Leadhills & Wanlockhead Railway, Leadhills
2'	E	1,200yds	NS886145	01573 223691

Strathaven Miniature Railway, George Allan Park, Strathaven
5"/7¼"	O	508yds	NS700448	01357 521995

WEST LOTHIAN
Almondell Model Engineering Centre, Broxburn
7¼"	O	1,100yds	NT084702	♦	Open days ⑨

Almond Valley Heritage Centre, Livingston
2' 6"	E	450yds	NT033669	♠	01506 414957

⑧ 31 March, 26 May, 28 July, 25 August
⑨ 5 May, 9 June, 3/4 August, 15 September

WALES

BRIDGEND
Bridgend Miniature Railway, Parc Slip Nature Park, Tondu
| 5"/7¼" | O | 840yds | SS882843 | ♣ | 07913 647764 |

Garw Valley Miniature Railway, Pontycymer
| 10¼" | E | 104yds | SS904912 | ♦ | Open days: 3 per year |

CARDIFF
Heath Park Miniature Railway, Heath
| 5"/7¼" | O | 400yds | ST178799 | ♣ | 029 2025 5000 |

CARMARTHENSHIRE
Gwili Miniature Railway, Llwyfan Cerrig, Gwili Steam Railway
| 7¼" | E | 235yds | SN405258 | ♣ | 01267 238213 |

Llanelli Model Engineers, Pembrey Country Park, Pembrey
| 5"/7¼" | O | 550yds | SN402002 | | Apr-Sep: Sundays |

CEREDIGION
Teifi Valley Railway, Henllan, Newcastle Emlyn
Main Line
| 2' | E | 970yds | SN359407 | | 01559 371077 |

Miniature Railway
| 7¼" | E | 300yds | SN359407 | | 01559 371077 |

Vale of Rheidol Railway, Aberystwyth
| 1' 11½" | E | 11¾ miles | SN585816 | T | 01970 625819 |

CONWY
Conwy Valley Railway, Railway Museum, Betws-y-Coed
| 7¼" | C | 950yds | SH796565 | | 01690 710568 |

DENBIGHSHIRE
Rhyl Miniature Railway, Marine Lake, Rhyl
| 15" | O | 1 mile | SH999807 | | 01352 759109(e) |

GWYNEDD
Bala Lake Railway, Llanuwchllyn, Bala
| 1' 11½" | E | 4½ miles | SH881300 | T | 01678 540666 |

Corris Railway, Corris, Machynlleth
| 2' 3" | E | 1,200yds | SH755078 | T | 01654 761303 |

Fairbourne Miniature Railway, Fairbourne
| 12¼" | E | 1¾ miles | SH615128 | T | 01341 250362 |

Ffestiniog & Welsh Highland Railways, Porthmadog
Ffestiniog Railway
| 1' 11½" | E | 13½ miles | SH571384 | T | 01766 516024 |

Welsh Highland Railway
| 1' 11½" | E | 24¾ miles | SH571384 | T | 01766 516024 |

Gypsy Wood Railway, Bontnewydd, Caernarfon
| 10¼" | B | 350yds | SH487603 | ♠ | 01286 673133 |

Llanberis Lake Railway, Gilfach Ddu, Llanberis
| 1' 11½" | E | 2½ miles | SH586604 | T | 01286 870549 |

GWYNEDD (Continued)

Snowdon Mountain Railway, Llanberis

2' 7½"	E	4¾ miles	SH582597	T		01286 870223

Talyllyn Railway, Tywyn

2' 3"	E	7¼ miles	SH586004	T		01654 710472

Welsh Highland Heritage Railway, Porthmadog
Main Line

1' 11½"	E	850yds	SH567392	T		01766 513402

Porthmadog Woodland Railway

7¼"	C	389yds	SH570392			01766 513402

MERTHYR TYDFIL

Brecon Mountain Railway, Pant, Merthyr Tydfil

1' 11¾"	E	4½ miles	SO059097	T		01685 722988

Cyfarthfa Park Miniature Railway, Cyfarthfa Castle Park, Merthyr Tydfil

5"/7¼"	O	330yds	SO041072			07815 521640

MONMOUTHSHIRE

Tintern Miniature Railway, The Old Station, Tintern

10¼"	E	180yds	SO537006			01291 689566

NEATH PORT TALBOT

Margam Park Railway, Margam Country Park, Port Talbot

2'	D	1¼ miles	SS802860	♠		01639 881635

NEWPORT

Cefn Mably Railway, Cefn Mably Farm Park, Michaelston-y-Fedw

12¼"	D	640yds	ST231843	♠		01633 680312

Newport Model Engineers, North Glebelands, Newport

5"/7¼"	C	600yds	ST320901	♣		07774 448631

PEMBROKESHIRE

Oakwood Main Line Train, Oakwood Theme Park, Cross Hands, Narberth

15"	O	1,100yds	SN069124	♠		01834 815170

POWYS

Mid Wales Model Engineers, Back Lane Park, Newtown

5"/7¼"	O	165yds	SO106915			01686 630757(e)

Welshpool & Llanfair Light Railway, Llanfair Caereinion

2' 6"	E	8 miles	SJ106068	T		01938 810441

SECTION 3
TRAMWAYS

All **Tramways** offering rides to the general public are contained in this section. The short, steeply inclined lines - "Cliff Railways" - can be found in Section 4. The section is divided by geographical area: Southern England, Midlands & Eastern England, Northern England, Isle of Man, Wales, Scotland.

Trams running through the streets of our towns and cities were once a common enough sight, but are now restricted to Douglas, Blackpool and Llandudno, although they have now made a comeback in the form of Light Railways in such cities as Manchester, Sheffield, Birmingham and Edinburgh. The first street Tramway was in Liverpool and opened in March 1859, but was short lived. Blackpool is very much the home of the British Tramway - the first electrically powered Trams, in the country, ran here in September 1885. Operation has been continuous since then, a situation unique in the British Isles. The earliest form of motive power used by the Tramways, the horse, is still represented at Douglas on the Isle of Man.

Each entry has six columns associated with it:

Column 1   Gauge in feet(') and inches(").

Column 2   Layout (as section 2, page 11).

Column 3   Route length of line in miles or yards, as available to passengers.

Column 4   Motive power employed.

Column 5   Ordnance Survey National Grid Reference. Reference refers to the main station or boarding point.

Column 6   Telephone number for enquires.
               ① Local Tourist Information Office. (e) Evenings only.

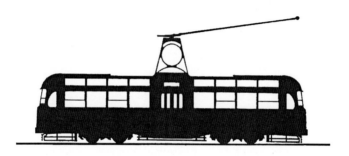

SOUTHERN ENGLAND

Seaton Tramway, Harbour Road, Seaton, Devon

2' 9"	E	2¾ miles	Electric	SY247901	01297 20375

Hill Train, Legoland, Windsor, Berkshire

3' 6"	E	550yds	Cable	SU937748	0871 222 2001

MIDLANDS & EASTERN ENGLAND

Black Country Living Museum, Tipton Road, Dudley, West Midlands

3' 6"	E	525yds	Electric	SO950914	0121 557 9643

Statfold Barn Tramway, Tamworth, Staffordshire

3'/4 8½"	E	600yds	Battery	SK242065	01827 830389

Crich Tramway Village, Crich, Derbyshire

4' 8½"	E	1,500yds	Electric	SK345549	01773 854321

East Anglia Transport Museum, Carlton Colville, Lowestoft, Suffolk

4' 8½"	E	400yds	Electric	TM506902	01502 518459

NORTHERN ENGLAND

Wirral Heritage Tramway, Woodside Ferry, Birkenhead, Merseyside

4' 8½"	E	950yds	Electric	SJ329892	0151 647 2128

Heaton Park Tramway, Prestwich, Greater Manchester

4' 8½"	E	940yds	Electric	SD835040	0161 740 1919

Shipley Glen Tramway, Saltaire, West Yorkshire

20"	E	386yds	Cable	SE139385	01274 589010

Beamish - The Living Museum of the North, Stanley, Durham

4' 8½"	O	1½ miles	Electric	NZ219542	0191 370 4000

ISLE OF MAN

Douglas Horse Tramway, Promenade, Douglas

3'	E	1 mile	Horse	SC395774	01624 696420

WALES

Heath Park Tramway, Heath, Cardiff

18"	E	260yds	Electric	ST178799	029 2025 5000

Great Orme Tramway, Llandudno, Conwy
Lower Section

3' 6"	E	872yds	Cable	SH778827	01492 577877

Upper Section

3' 6"	E	827yds	Cable	SH766833	01492 577877

SCOTLAND

Summerlee Museum of Scottish Industrial Life, Coatbridge, North Lanarkshire

4' 8½"	E	500yds	Electric	NS729654	01236 638460

CairnGorm Mountain Railway, Aviemore, Highland

6' 6"	E	1¼ miles	Cable	NH990060	01479 861261

SECTION 4
CLIFF RAILWAYS

All public **Cliff Railways** are included in this section, but not vertical lifts like that at Whitby. Some information such as length and gauge, vary between sources. Where differences exist, the information given here is that quoted by the Railway itself. The section is divided by geographical area: Southern England, Midlands & Eastern England, Northern England, Wales.

Cliff Railways seem rarely to receive much attention from the average enthusiast, but short as they are, their history, operation and technology can be of much interest. The first Cliff Railway to be built in the British Isles was the line at South Cliff, Scarborough, which opened on 6th July 1875 at a cost of £8,000! Other lines followed, the majority being at seaside resorts. The exceptions are those at Bridgnorth and the line into the deep mine at the Llechwedd Slate Caverns. The railways use a variety of gauges, with the widest being on the West Hill Railway in Hastings and the steepest gradient being on the East Hill Railway in the same Sussex town.

Each entry has six columns associated with it:

Column 1   Gauge in feet(') and inches(").

Column 2   Layout: D - Double track. S - Single track.

Column 3   Length of track in feet (actual length of track NOT height).

Column 4   Gradient of line, stated as track length against height attained.

Column 5   Ordnance Survey National Grid Reference.

Column 6   Telephone number for enquires.
             ① Local Tourist Information Office. (e) Evenings only.

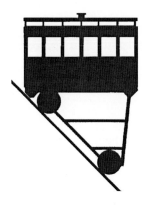

SOUTHERN ENGLAND
Lynton & Lynmouth, Devon

| 3' 9" | D | 862' | 1 in 1.75 | SS720496 | 01598 753486 |

Babbacombe Cliff, Torquay, Devon

| 5' 8" | D | 716' | 1 in 2.83 | SX924657 | 01803 328750 |

West Cliff, Bournemouth, Dorset

| 5' 6" | D | 145' | 1 in 1.42 | SZ085906 | 01202 451781 |

Fishermans Walk, Pokesdown, Dorset

| 5' 8" | D | 128' | 1 in 1.49 | SZ130913 | 01202 451781 |

West Hill, Hastings, East Sussex

| 6' | D | 500' | 1 in 3 | TQ822094 | 01424 451111 |

East Hill, Hastings, East Sussex

| 5' | D | 267' | 1 in 1.28 | TQ827095 | 01424 451111 |

Southend, Essex

| 4' 6" | S | 130' | 1 in 2.3 | TQ881851 | 01702 618747 |

MIDLANDS & EASTERN ENGLAND
Castle Hill, Bridgnorth, Shropshire

| 3' 8" | D | 201' | 1 in 1.8 | SO718930 | 01746 762052 |

NORTHERN ENGLAND
South Cliff, Scarborough, North Yorkshire

| 4' 8½" | D | 284' | 1 in 1.75 | TA045877 | 01723 372351 |

Central Cliff, Scarborough, North Yorkshire

| 4' 8½" | D | 234' | 1 in 2 | TA044884 | 01723 501754 |

Saltburn, North Yorkshire

| 4' 2½" | D | 207' | 1 in 1.7 | NZ666217 | 01287 622528 |

WALES
Constitution Hill, Aberystwyth, Ceredigion

| 4' 10" | D | 778' | 1 in 2 | SN584826 | 01970 617642 |

Llechwedd Slate Caverns, Blaenau Ffestiniog, Gwynedd

| 3' | S | 420' | 1 in 1.8 | SH699470 | 01766 830306 |

CHANGES SINCE 35th EDITION - SUPPLEMENT 3

To enable readers to keep track of changes (new entries, extensions and closures) between editions, the list below details changes that have taken place since the 3rd supplement to the 35th edition was published. Opening and closure dates are shown where known.

New Entries
None

Extensions
Mease Valley Light Railway: Extension opened 16/03/24

Closures
Saughtree Station: Station sold 29/09/23
Greenham Paddock Railway: Line out of use. Did not run in 2023
Churwell Woodland Railway: Line closed 10/2023. Lifted by 04/12/23
Centre for Alternative Technology: Centre closed to day visitors 09/11/23

BRANCH LINE SOCIETY

Object
The object of the **Branch Line Society**, formed in 1955, is to promote and encourage the study of railway systems with particular reference to branch lines. The society arranges tours over, and visits to, railway systems and places of railway interest. A newsletter - *Branch Line News* - is published (in both paper & electronic format) 24 times a year and this features a *Minor Railways* column which is linked to the book you are reading. This column provides reports from members, additional information and up to date news about all minor railways.

Membership Enquiries
For membership enquiries contact:
Membership Secretary, 186 Anlaby Park Road South, Hull, HU4 7BU.
membership.secretary@branchline.uk.

Web Site
www.branchline.uk.

FURTHER READING & INFORMATION

There are many books available with information about minor railways. A small selection is listed below and these can be recommended:

Steam Heritage - Annual publication listing most minor railways, museums & special events
Steam Heritage Publishing 2024. ISSN 0269 2368.

Still Steaming - A list of 100 minor railways where "steam still lives".
Soccer Books Limited 2023. ISBN 978 1 86223 498 7.

Industrial Locomotives 18EL - Lists all locomotives, 15" gauge and over
Industrial Railway Society 2019. ISBN 978 1 901556 99 5.

Miniature Railways of Great Britain & Ireland - Good guide to miniature railways and their locomotives, from 21" gauge down to 7¼" gauge
Platform 5 Publishing 2012. ISBN 978 1 902336 93 0.

Miniature Steam Railway Locomotives in the British Isles - Lists all steam locomotives between 7¼" and 16" gauges. Locomotives are listed by builder and current location
LCGB 2009.

Narrow Gauge Steam Locomotives of Great Britain & Ireland - Good guide to narrow gauge locomotives, from 1' 6" to 4' 6" gauge.
Platform 5 Publishing 2014. ISBN 978 1 909431 11 9.

Cliff Railways of the British Isles - Excellent book detailing the history of our cliff railways
The Oakwood Press 2002. ISBN 0 85361 594 2.

Railway Modeller - Annual guide to railway attractions. Very useful
Peco Publications (Published with June *Railway Modeller*). ISSN 0033 8931.

Miniature Railway - Excellent quarterly magazine devoted to miniature railways
A to B Magazines. ISSN 1751 3103.

The following Societies produce newsletters and magazines with news and information on minor railways (see also **Minor Railways *online*** Links page):

Narrow Gauge Railway Society
4 Barnside Way, Moulton, CW9 8PT

Industrial Railway Society
24 Dulverton Road, Melton Mowbray, LE13 0SF

Heywood Society
52 Cheswick Way, Cheswick Green, Solihull, B90 4HE

7¼" Gauge Society
14 Moorcroft, Eldwick, Bingley, BD16 3DR